MY WORLD OF SCIENCE

# Hot and Cold

### Revised and Updated

Angela Royston

**www.heinemann.co.uk/library**
Visit our website to find out more information about Heinemann Library books.

To order:
☎ Phone 44 (0) 1865 888066 ·
🖹 Send a fax to 44 (0) 1865 314091
🖥 Visit the Heinemann Bookshop at www.heinemann.co.uk/library to browse our catalogue and order online.

First published in Great Britain by Heinemann Library, Halley Court, Jordan Hill, Oxford OX2 8EJ, part of Pearson Education. Heinemann is a registered trademark of Pearson Education Ltd.

Editorial: Diyan Leake
Design: Joanna Hinton-Malivoire
Picture research: Melissa Allison and Mica Brancic
Production: Duncan Gilbert

Originated by Chroma Graphics (Overseas) Pte Ltd
Printed and bound in China by South China Printing Co. Ltd

ISBN 978 0 431 13761 2 (hardback)
12 11 10 09 08
10 9 8 7 6 5 4 3 2 1

ISBN 978 0 431 13785 8 (paperback)
12 11 10 09 08
10 9 8 7 6 5 4 3 2 1

**British Library Cataloguing in Publication Data**
Royston, Angela
  Hot and cold. – New ed. – (My world of science)
  1. Temperature – Juvenile literature  2. Cold
  – Juvenile literature
  3. Heat – Juvenile literature  I. Title
  536.5

**Acknowledgements**
The publishers would like to thank the following for permission to reproduce photographs: © Eye Ubiquitous p. 7 (Sylvia Greenland); © Getty Images pp. 5 (Stockfood Creative), **15**; © Masterfile p. **22** (Boden/Ledingha); © Robert Harding pp. **4**, **8**; © Science Photo Library pp. **9** (Geoff Tompkinson), **14**; © Trevor Clifford pp. **6**, **10**, **11**, **12**, **13**, **16**, **17**, **19**, **20**, **21**, **23**, **24**, **25**, **26**, **27**, **28**, **29**; Trip p. **18** (H. Rogers).

Cover photograph reproduced with permission of © Masterfile (Janet Foster).

The publishers would like to thank Jon Bliss for his assistance in the preparation of this book.

Every effort has been made to contact copyright holders of any material reproduced in this book. Any omissions will be rectified in subsequent printings if notice is given to the publishers.

# Contents

Any words appearing in the text in bold, **like this**, are explained in the glossary.

# Hot and cold

Some things are hot. When food is very hot, you can see **steam** rising from it. You need to be careful not to burn your mouth when you eat it.

This jacket potato is very hot.

Other things are very cold. As you lick a frozen juice lolly, it makes your lips and tongue cold, too.

# Danger!

Many things may be so hot they can burn and hurt you. A cooker may be very hot.

People use oven gloves to help protect their hands from very hot pans.

Keep away from hot things even when they are turned off. A hot iron smoothes out creases in clothes. It stays hot for a long time after it has been turned off.

# Neither hot nor cold

Some things are neither hot nor cold.
The water in a swimming pool can be
cool, warm, or **lukewarm**.

This baby's bathwater is warmer than the water in a swimming pool. But it is probably cooler than your bathwater.

# Temperature

We use words like warm, cool, hot, and cold to talk about **temperature**. The boy in the picture is testing the temperature of the bathwater with his hand.

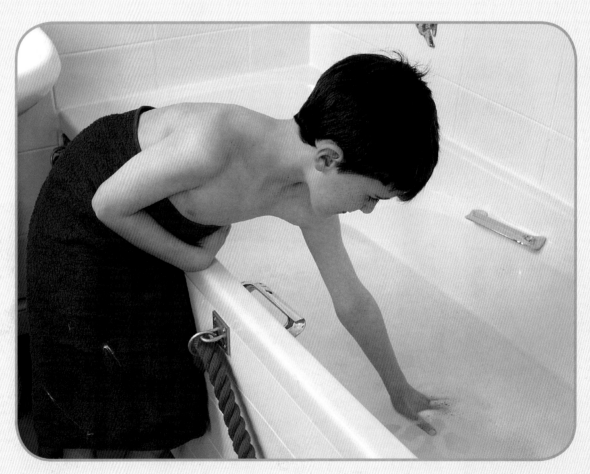

Different parts of the body feel temperature differently. The bathwater will probably feel hotter to the boy's foot than to his hand.

# Testing temperatures

**Temperatures** can feel different when you are hot or cold. The girl is holding her hands in warm water. The boy is holding his hands in cold water.

| warm water | cold water |

lukewarm water

Now they both put their hands in **lukewarm** water. The girl says it feels cool. The boy says it feels warm.

# Thermometers

A **thermometer measures** exactly how hot or cold something is. This doctor is using a thermometer to measure the **temperature** of the girl's body.

Temperature is measured in **degrees Celsius**, or **°C**. Normal temperature for people is 37 °C.

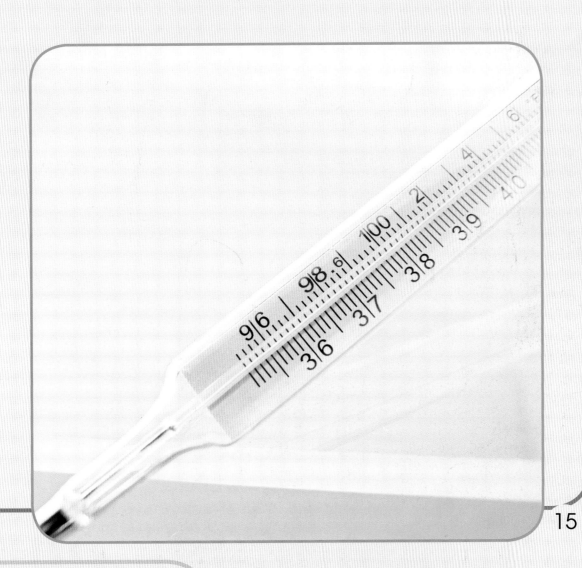

# More thermometers

This **thermometer measures** the **temperature** of the air in a room. It shows 20 **degrees Celsius (°C)**. The room will be nice and warm.

This thermometer measures the temperature of the air outside. A temperature of 30 °C is very hot. But 5 °C is very cold.

# Keeping cool

In hot weather we dress to keep ourselves as cool as possible. Many people wear light, loose clothes. These protect them from the sun.

These people live in a very hot place.

Wind can make you feel cooler. This girl
is holding a fan which makes a wind. The
wind cools her down.

# Keeping warm

Hats, gloves, and coats keep cold air out. What special clothes are these children putting on to keep warm? (Answer on page 31.)

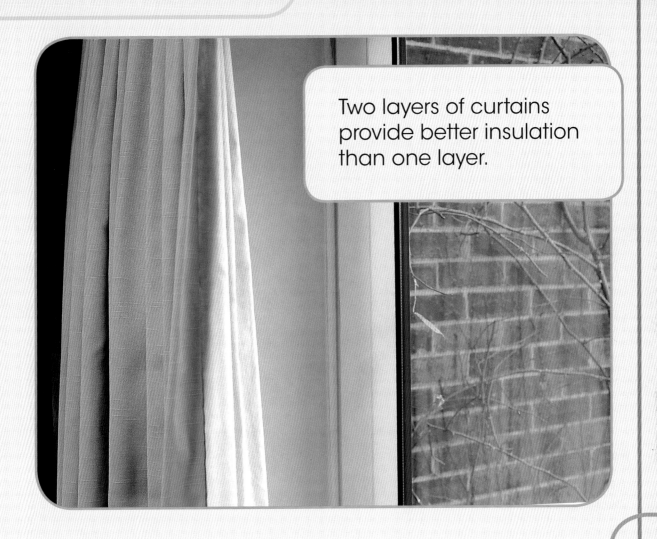

Two layers of curtains provide better insulation than one layer.

**Insulation** keeps warm air in and cold air out. Windows may have two layers of glass to keep the heat in. Curtains help to **insulate** the house as well.

# Cooking

Water is heated to make it boil.

Some food must be cooked to make it safe to eat. When water is heated to 100 **degrees Celsius**, it is at its boiling point.

This girl is making a cake. She stirs the **ingredients** which make a runny **liquid** mixture. When the mixture is cooked in a hot oven, it turns **solid**.

# Fridges

A fridge keeps food colder than the air in the room does. The temperature in a fridge is just above the **freezing point** of water.

When food is stored in a cold fridge, it stays **fresh** for longer.

The bottom of the fridge is the coldest part. But if there is a freezer **compartment**, it is even colder. What is stored in the coldest part of this fridge? (Answer on page 31.)

# Freezing

A freezer keeps food even colder than a fridge. The temperature of a freezer is below 0 **degrees Celsius (°C)**, which is the **freezing point** of water.

Ice cubes melt when they are taken out of the freezer and put into warmer drinks.

This boy is putting a tray of water into the freezer. The water will get colder. When it reaches 0 °C, it will turn into **solid** ice cubes.

# Melting

This boy is enjoying an ice cream. As the cold ice cream becomes warmer, it starts to melt. It changes from **solid** spoonfuls into a runny **liquid**.

Chocolate should not be melted straight in a pan, but in a bowl over hot water.

If you heat chocolate, it will start to melt. When the chocolate cools down, it becomes solid again.

# Glossary

**compartment** small box

**degrees Celsius (°C)** units of measurement on a thermometer

**freezing point** temperature at which a liquid becomes a solid

**fresh** nice to eat, not old

**ingredients** the different parts of a mixture

**insulate** stop heat or cold from passing through

**insulation** a material that keeps heat in and cold out

**liquid** stuff that can flow, such as water or oil

**lukewarm** slightly warm

**measure** find out how big, heavy, hot or cold something is

**solid** something that has a fixed shape and is not a liquid or a gas

**steam** tiny droplets of very hot water that float in the air

**temperature** how hot or cold something is

**thermometer** tool that measures temperature

# Answers

**Page 20 –** The children are putting on coats, hats, scarves, gloves and heavy shoes to keep warm.

**Page 25 –** Vegetables, milk, and juice are stored in the coldest part of the fridge.

# More books to read

*Heat: Too Hot or Too Cold?* Sally Hewitt (Stargazer Books, 2006)

*I Know Opposites: Hot and Cold,* Gini Holland (Gareth Stevens, 2007)

*Science In Your Life – Hot and Cold: Feel It!* Wendy Sadler (Raintree, 2006)

# Index